Howell Mountain School

Amazing Grace

AMAZING GRACE

The Story Behind the Song

JIM HASKINS

The Millbrook Press
Brookfield, Connecticut

I am grateful to Kathy Benson, Ann Kalkahoff,
Emily Lewis, Bill Rice, and Mrs. Elizabeth Knight,
vice-chairman of the trustees of the
Cowper and Newton Museum, for their help.

Illustrations and photographs courtesy of the Library
of Congress: pp. 12, 32, 34, 43; The Granger
Collection: pp. 15, 18; Bettmann Archive: p. 17;
North Wind Picture Archives: pp. 22, 23, 25, 27,
31, 38, 40; New York Public Library Picture Collection: p. 36; Christian Steiner/Philips Classics: p. 45.

Library of Congress Cataloging-in-Publication Data
Haskins, James, 1941–
Amazing grace: the story behind the song / by Jim Haskins
p.   cm.
Includes index.
Summary: Relates the story of the British slave trader who
rejected his calling, became a minister, and wrote the words to
the popular hymn "Amazing Grace."
ISBN 1-56294-117-8
1. Newton, John, 1725–1807—Juvenile literature.   2. Amazing grace
(Hymn)—Juvenile literature.   3. Hymn writers—England—Biography—
Juvenile literature.   [1. Newton, John, 1725–1807.   2. Hymn
writers.   3. Clergy.   4. Amazing grace (Hymn)]   I. Title.
BV330.N48H37   1992
264'.2'092—dc20
[B]   91-20999 CIP AC

To Will and Jane

Contents

Amazing Grace

Amazing grace (how sweet the sound)
That saved a wretch like me!
I once was lost, but now am found,
Was blind, but now I see.

A Song of Hope

Have you ever felt sad and hopeless? Have you ever felt "wretched"? You are not alone. Nobody is happy all the time. But for over two hundred years people have sung or listened to "Amazing Grace" to feel better.

"Amazing Grace" is a song of hope. It says that no matter how wretched you feel, there is a chance to feel better. The song tells about grace as God's love and protection.

"Amazing Grace" was written as a hymn by John Newton, an English minister, in the 1760s. Around 1900, the words of the hymn were published with an American melody. No one knows exactly when, but at some point "Amazing Grace" became a kind of folk song as well as a hymn.

People do not have to be religious to love "Amazing Grace." Many people have been comforted by the simple words and beautiful melody.

John Newton wrote the words for "Amazing Grace" more than two hundred years ago. Ever since then, people have found hope in this lovely folk hymn.

The Reverend John Newton believed in God most of his life. But that did not keep him from having troubles and sorrows. Many times he felt very wretched. When he was old, he was amazed that he had survived to find the grace of God. This is his story, as well as the story of "Amazing Grace."

'Twas grace that taught my heart to fear,
And grace my fears relieved;
How precious did that grace appear
The hour I first believed!

John Newton's Early Years

John Newton was born in London, England, in 1725. His father was a ship captain who was often away from home. His mother was a religious woman. She taught little John about God when he was very young. He felt happy to know that there was a God who would protect him.

John's mother read the Bible to him often. He could read by himself by the time he was four. He wasn't even six years old when she started to teach him arithmetic and Latin. But sadly, John's mother died before he was seven.

John's father soon married again. But John did not get to spend much time with his stepmother. In England, boys of well-to-do parents were sent away to boarding school at a young age. John was sent to a school in Essex, England.

Discipline was strict in English schools of the 1700s. Here, a teacher, or master, prepares to use a switch on an unruly student.

The masters at the school were very strict. They made learning seem like a punishment. John hated the school and was glad when his father took him out.

Next, John went to sea with his father. On the ship, John learned about navigation. He learned about how a sailing ship depended on the wind. If the wind was blowing nicely, the voyage was easy. If there was little wind, the ship was "becalmed" and hardly moved at all. If there was a storm at sea, the ship was tossed about on the waves like a toy and everyone was in danger. John visited many ports along the Mediterranean Sea. He learned that there was a big world outside of England.

But John wasn't very happy during his travels. His father was not warm and loving as his mother had been. Instead, Captain Newton was stern and distant. John didn't feel that his father cared very much about him. He acted up a lot in order to get his father's attention.

After sailing with his father for five years, John became an apprentice to a Spanish merchant. His father believed that John would learn more and become more independent if he were taught the merchant trade. But John was more interested in getting into mischief than learning a trade. He soon lost that job.

John remembered how safe he had felt when his mother had taught him about God. He no longer felt so protected. He also feared that his mischief-making would keep him from God's love and forgiveness forever.

John tried many ways to find God's grace. He tried praying. He tried going without meat. He kept long silences. But when nothing worked, he was angry. He turned against his

London was a busy port when John Newton went to sea. From this wharf, trading ships set sail for ports all over the world.

This print from the 1700s shows a man being dragged off to serve in the British Royal Navy. At the time, navy "press-gangs" like the one shown here were allowed to kidnap any healthy man without a job.

religion and refused to pray. John started getting into trouble again.

His father didn't know what to do with him. Then a merchant friend offered to send John to the island of Jamaica for five years to learn the plantation business. His father thought that would be a good thing for John. John did not care what he did, and he didn't think he had much choice anyway.

Before he left for Jamaica, in the West Indies, John decided to visit some friends of his mother's. There, he fell in love with their oldest daughter, Mary Catlett. She was no more than fourteen, and he was only seventeen. They were too young to get serious about their love. But John could not bring himself to leave Mary and meet the ship bound for Jamaica. He missed the boat.

John's angry father then signed him up for duty on a merchant ship bound for the Mediterranean Sea. John was gone nearly a year. As soon as he got back to England, he went to visit Mary. Again, he stayed longer than he should have and missed the next ship on which he was supposed to sail.

John was in London trying to get another job on a ship when he was kidnapped! At that time, the British Royal Navy was allowed to kidnap any healthy man without a job and order him into service. Britain was about to go to war with France, and the navy needed sailors. John served on the H.M.S. (Her Majesty's Ship) *Harwich* for two years.

When John was nearly twenty, he learned that the *Harwich* was going on a five-year cruise to the East Indies. He did not want to be away from Mary that long, so he tried to escape. But he was caught and put in iron shackles below deck. Then he was brought up on deck, stripped to the waist, and whipped.

John was still determined to avoid that long voyage. Luckily, the *Harwich* met a slave-trading ship that wanted to exchange men. The captain of the trader had two men he could not control. He asked the captain of the *Harwich* to take them. In return, he wanted two men from the *Harwich.* John pleaded with his captain to let him go to the slave trader. The captain was glad to be rid of him. And so, young John Newton entered the African slave trade.

Through many dangers, toils, and snares
I have already come;
'Tis grace has brought me safe thus far,
And grace will lead me home.

Slave Trader

In those days, few people saw anything wrong with the slave trade. Slaves were not treated like human beings. Instead, they were thought of as goods or property. In England, only the Quakers objected to this. But not many people paid attention to the Quakers, a religious group that had practices and beliefs that were considered strange.

European countries like England and Portugal had colonies in the Americas. These colonies needed workers for their plantations and mines. African chiefs were willing to sell slaves to the Europeans in exchange for goods like iron, guns, and cloth. The European colonies in the Americas had rum, sugar, and cotton to trade for slaves.

European slave ships took goods to Africa to exchange for slaves. The ships left Africa loaded with slaves. They headed

Captives were marched to the African coast to be sold as slaves. They were chained together on the long march so that they would not run away.

for the Americas to trade the slaves for goods produced in the colonies. The ships then returned to Europe loaded with those goods.

For John Newton, being on a slave trader was much better than being in the British Royal Navy. But he still did not behave. He had a good sense of humor and was well liked by the crew. But the ship's officers did not think much of him.

They especially did not like John after he made up a song that poked fun at them. Soon, all the crew members were singing it.

When the ship reached Africa, John got a job with an Englishman who lived on one of the Plantane islands off the coast. This man gathered slaves to be sold to the ships. The man lived with an African woman who did not like John. When the man went away to search for slaves, the woman

At the coast, the slaves were held in sheds like this one until a slave ship came to buy them.

treated John very cruelly. He had to work with the slaves on a lime-tree plantation without pay. He was poorly fed and clothed. John later wrote that he was "rather pitied than scorned by the meanest [lowest] of her slaves."

When the trader returned, he did not believe John's stories of poor treatment. Instead, he treated John as badly as his wife had. He took John on his next voyage in search of slaves. But he did not trust John. Whenever the master left the ship, he locked John in irons on the deck, with only a little rice to eat. It was the rainy season, and John sometimes spent thirty or forty hours out in the rain.

Fortunately for John, another English trader arrived on the island. John's master was ashamed of being seen treating a fellow Englishman like a slave. He released John to go to work for the new trader. John and another white servant were sent to manage a slave "factory," where slaves were brought and held for sale to the slave ships.

John was still a servant, but he was free to travel about. He went up and down the rivers buying slaves. He got to know the Africans there very well. John found them to be much more honest and trusting than the English. He later wrote, "I have lived long, and conversed [talked] much, amongst these supposed savages. I have often slept in their towns, in a house filled with goods for trade, with no person in the house but myself, and with no other door than a mat."

Africa's rivers provided routes for the slave trade. Here, slavers bring captives to market by canoe.

John also wrote that any dishonesty he found in the Africans was a result of dealing with Europeans: "The most humane and moral people I ever met in Africa were on the River Gaboon and at Cape Lopas; and they were the people who had the least intercourse [contact] with Europe."

John was happy doing his job. When a slave-ship captain arrived with word that John's father had been searching for him, John almost did not want to leave.

His father had been very worried about him. In fact, Captain Newton was afraid his son was dead. He had asked the slave-ship captain to find John and bring him back no matter what. John did not want to go back to England because of his father. But he did want to see Mary. So he went with the captain. It was February 1747. After fifteen months as a slave and servant, John Newton was now free.

The slave-ship captain was on a trading voyage. Thus, it would be another year before John reached England. John didn't have to do any work on the trip, and he soon got into trouble. One night he and some other sailors got drunk. His hat fell overboard, and he nearly drowned trying to get it back. Another time he and a few others went ashore to hunt and got lost. It took hours to find their way back to the ship. The captain was losing patience with John.

At last, the ship set sail for England. Off the banks of Newfoundland, in North America, a violent storm arose. The sea tore away the upper timbers of the ship, and it was in danger of sinking. John and the crew spent hours pumping water out of the hold. Tired and afraid, John heard himself say, "If this will not do, the Lord have mercy on us!" He had not asked God for anything in years.

A slave ship caught in a violent storm. John Newton was lucky that his ship weathered a similar storm. When a slave ship sank, the chained captives it carried were almost certain to die.

The storm ended. By the following day the crew had managed to pump out all the water on the ship. John started to think about the religion that he had once believed in so firmly. He thought about the bad things he had done in his life. John became very afraid. He later wrote, "I thought that if the Christian religion were true, I could not be forgiven, and therefore was expecting, and almost at times wishing, to know the worst."

There were more troubles to come. Food supplies ran low. The crew had to pump all the time to keep the ship free of water. The storm had thrown the ship way off course. To make matters worse, the captain had decided that John was somehow to blame for all the troubles. But at last they sighted Ireland and anchored.

Wrote John Newton, "When we came into this port, our very last victuals [food] were boiling in the pot. Before we had been there two hours, the wind began to blow with great violence. If we had continued at sea that night in our shattered, enfeebled condition, we would to all human appearance, have gone to the bottom. *About this time I began to know that there is a God who hears every prayer.*"

While in Ireland, John wrote home. By that time, his father had given him up for lost. The older man must have been overjoyed to hear that his son was safe. But he was sad that John could not go with him on his next voyage. John's father was about to leave for Hudson Bay in North America to be the governor of York Fort. He had wanted John to go with him. But his ship sailed before John returned to England.

John looked forward to seeing his father again. He wanted to ask the older man's forgiveness for all the trouble he had caused. But his father drowned in North America in 1751. John never saw him again.

The Lord has promised good to me,
His word my hope secures;
He will my shield and portion be
As long as life endures.

Christian Slave Trader

Before John's father had left for Hudson Bay, he had given his consent for John to marry Mary Catlett. Her parents also gave their consent, and John and Mary became engaged. At that time, he was twenty-three years old and she was twenty.

Before they could marry, John felt he needed to make enough money to support a wife. Mary agreed to wait while John made another voyage to the west coast of Africa. He would serve as first mate to the captain of the ship that had taken John to England from Ireland.

In Africa, they loaded a cargo of slaves and were about to set sail for the West Indies. All that remained was to bring wood and water from shore. John was all set to go ashore in the small boat to get the supplies when the captain called him back. John could not understand why he was called back, and

Many slaves were shipped to the American colonies. This open shed served as a slave market in colonial New York.

the captain could not explain it either. But that night, the small boat sank. John was certain it was another act of God's grace.

When the ship finally returned to England, John went to Mary as soon as he could. They were married on February 12,

Negroes for Sale.

A Cargo of very fine stout Men and Women, in good order and fit for immediate service, just imported from the Windward Coast of Africa, in the Ship Two Brothers.—

Conditions are one half Cash or Produce, the other half payable the first of January next, giving Bond and Security if required.

The Sale to be opened at 10 o'Clock each Day, in Mr. Bourdeaux's Yard, at No. 48, on the Bay.

May 19, 1784. JOHN MITCHELL.

Thirty Seasoned Negroes

To be Sold for Credit, at Private Sale.

AMONGST which is a Carpenter, none of whom are known to be dishonest.

Also, to be sold for Cash, a regular bred young Negroe Man-Cook, born in this Country, who served several Years under an exceeding good French Cook abroad, and his Wife a middle aged Washer-Woman, (both very honest) and their two Children. *Likewise,* a young Man a Carpenter.

For Terms apply to the Printer.

Newspapers advertised slaves for sale.

1750. The following August, John set sail for Africa again. This time he was the commander of a ship.

John Newton knew how much his life had changed in such a short time. He wrote to his wife in September 1751, "My condition when abroad . . . might be envied by multitudes who stay at home. . . . If I say to one, Come, he comes; if to another, Go, he flies. If I order one person to do something, perhaps three or four will be ambitious of a share in the service. Not a man must eat his dinner until I please give him leave; nay, nobody dares to say it is twelve or eight o'clock in my hearing, till I think proper to say it first. . . . But in the midst of all my parade, I do not forget (I hope I never shall) what my situation was on board the *Harwich* and at the Plantanes."

It was no easy job to command a slave-trading ship. There were many dangers. The crews of such ships were usually treated very badly. As a result, the men were hardened and very difficult to handle. Mutinies (rebellions) often occurred. A captain had to be very careful if he didn't want to find himself captured or thrown overboard.

A slave-ship captain also had to guard against mutinies among the slaves. John wrote, "It is always taken for granted, that they will attempt to gain their liberty if possible. . . . One unguarded hour, or minute, is sufficient to give the slaves the opportunity they are always looking for."

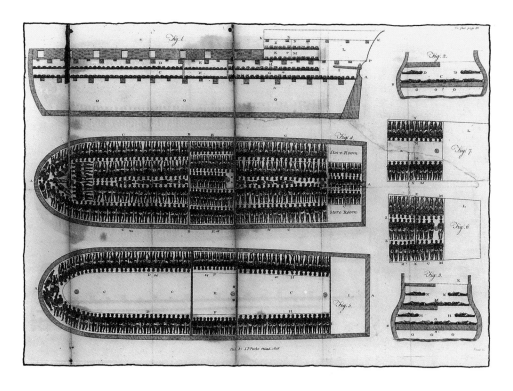

This diagram shows how tightly slaves were packed into the slave ships. The more slaves a ship carried, the more money the slave trader would make.

John had begun to pray and read his Bible again. He felt once more the protection and love of God, just as he had when he was a child. He tried to share his renewed sense of grace with others. He ordered that everyone on the ship should pray on Sunday. He held regular prayer services. John knew that the sailors cared most about the dangers and troubles they faced every day. So he made up prayers especially for them. In these prayers, he asked for God's protection from storms and other perils.

As for the slaves, John tried to treat them with as much kindness as he could. He later wrote that he treated the slaves, "while under my care, with as much humanity as a regard to my own safety would permit."

Many slave captains packed the ships so full with slaves that the slaves could barely move. John preferred to give them a little more space. Very few slave ships made it to the Americas without losing many of the slaves to sickness, suicide, or mutiny. On one of his voyages, John Newton did not lose a single slave. He was one of the few slave-ship captains in history to do so.

John made three voyages as the captain of a slave ship. He was about to set out on a fourth in early November 1754, when he came down with a fever. He could not make the voyage, and he decided not to try again.

He did not leave the slave trade because he believed it was wrong. But he later wrote, "I did see myself as a sort of jailer and I was sometimes shocked with an employment [work] that was perpetually [always] connected with chains, bolts, and shackles. In this view I had often prayed that the Lord in His

Sailors force slaves into a ship's hold. Slaves were kept in the dark hold for most of the long voyage.

own time would be pleased to place me in a more humane calling. . . . I longed to be freed from these long separations from home, which were very often hard to bear. My prayers were answered, though in a way I little expected."

Yes, when this flesh and heart shall fail,
And mortal life shall cease,
I shall possess, within the vail,
A life of joy and peace.

Christian Minister

John Newton got over his ailment. But then his wife, Mary, came down with it. John took care of Mary for nearly a year until she got better.

Then he got a job in the customs department of the government. During the years he held that post, he studied religion and decided to become a minister. In 1764, at the age of thirty-nine, he was ordained. He became a curate (minister) in the town of Olney. There, he met a poet named William Cowper. Cowper had just spent over a year in a hospital for the mentally ill. He had moved to Olney for peace and quiet. But his illness returned, and John took care of him for over a year.

During this time, the two talked often about religion. They decided to write some hymns that expressed how they felt about

William Cowper worked with John Newton on the Olney Hymns. Cowper later became one of the most famous English poets of his time.

God. These hymns came to be called the *Olney Hymns.* "Amazing Grace" was one of them.

In this hymn, John tried to share how grateful he was to God for letting him find grace when he had sinned so much. He also tried to express his joy at having found grace.

John Newton did not know when he wrote "Amazing Grace" that he would later feel very guilty about the part he had taken in the slave trade. In fact, at times he would wonder if he deserved the life of joy and peace that he talked about in "Amazing Grace."

But as John grew older, he thought about the dangers, toils, and snares he'd been through. He recalled the years when he did not pray. He remembered the time he was a slave. He thought about the time his ship almost sank. He realized his greatest sin had been taking part in the slave trade. He became ashamed of his part in a trade that enslaved other human beings.

By the late 1700s, many people in England were against slavery. They thought treating human beings like property or goods was evil. John Newton was among them. He said of the slave trade, "I hope it will always be a subject of humiliating reflection to me, that I was once an active instrument in a business at which my heart now shudders."

In 1788, he wrote a pamphlet called *Thoughts Upon the African Slave Trade.* In it he argued strongly against slavery.

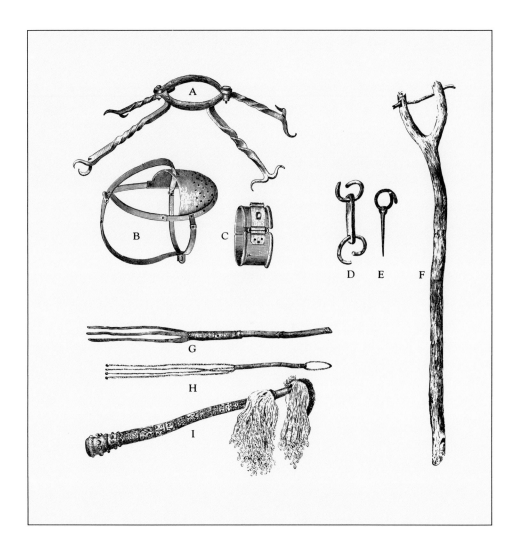

The brutality of the slave trade helped turn many people against it. These instruments were used to capture and subdue slaves. They include iron collars (A and C), an iron mask (B), wrist irons (D and E), a yoke (F), whips (G and H), and a club (I).

He also spoke to government committees that were trying to decide whether to outlaw the slave trade.

In fact, he spent much time toward the end of his life working to outlaw the slave trade. His shame at being part of it was one of several crosses he had to bear.

Another was the long illness of his adopted daughter, Elizabeth. And still another was the illness and death of his wife after they had been together forty years.

John himself died in 1807 at the age of eighty-two. He would have liked to see slavery abolished in England. But he did not live to see his wish come true. Slavery was not abolished until 1834. But John's writings helped to bring that about.

John Newton left behind shipboard logs, journals, autobiographies, and his pamphlet, *Thoughts Upon the African Slave Trade*. Together they make up one of the most detailed records of the slave trade that has ever existed. They are read today by people who study that history.

The hymn that John Newton left behind is very different from the sad story of the slave trade. The simple but beautiful "Amazing Grace," which tells of one man's joy at finding the grace of God, has brought hope to millions of people.

The earth shall soon dissolve like snow,
The sun forbear to shine;
But God, who call'd me here below,
Will be forever mine.

A Living Song

"Amazing Grace" has been sung in southern churches, especially black churches, as long as anyone can remember. But it has been sung not only in churches and at religious observances. The country-and-western singer Johnny Cash remembers that his family sang it while they were working in the cotton fields in Arkansas in the early part of this century. It has also been sung in prisons for many years.

In the early 1970s, folk songs were very popular. Folk singers like Judy Collins began to sing and record "Amazing Grace." In this way, many millions of people learned it.

Nowadays, "Amazing Grace" is often sung at special events. In 1990, the black opera singer Jessye Norman sang it at a rock concert in London. The concert was in honor of the seventieth birthday of Nelson Mandela, the black South Af-

"Amazing Grace" became a favorite hymn in black churches. This print shows a revival meeting in the 1800s.

rican freedom fighter. "Amazing Grace" was sung to honor Nelson Mandela for the pain he had suffered with grace and dignity during twenty-five years in prison. In 1991, the families of those serving in the Gulf War listened to "Amazing Grace" at prayer meetings.

"Amazing Grace" is loved by so many because its words are simple and honest. They could have come from the heart of any man, woman, or child. When people hear "Amazing Grace" for the first time, they feel as if they already know it.

"Amazing Grace" is very special to people who know the story of the man who wrote it. It is also special to people who feel they might never be forgiven. They know that John Newton found peace despite his part in the slave trade. So, too, can others be at peace about the wrong things they have done.

Over the years, people have added new verses to "Amazing Grace." Some people sing a verse that John Newton wrote for another hymn, called "The Name of Jesus":

> *How sweet the name of Jesus sounds*
> *In a believer's ear.*
> *It soothes his sorrows, heals his wounds,*
> *And drives away his fear.*

As a child, the singer Johnny Cash learned this verse, which is about heaven:

> *When we've been there ten thousand years,*
> *Bright shining as the sun;*
> *We've no less days to sing God's praise,*
> *Than when we first began.*

The opera star Jessye Norman is among many recent performers who have sung "Amazing Grace" in concert.

No one thinks John Newton would have minded. After all, adding new verses makes "Amazing Grace" a "living" song, one that changes as people need it to. John Newton would have liked the idea that a song he wrote more than two hundred years ago is probably more popular today than when he first wrote it.

In fact, that is *really* amazing!

Index